Poetry, My Bible, and Me

A book of poetry, based on scriptures, life, and thought.

RAYMOND K. HUFF

iUniverse, Inc.
New York   Bloomington

iUniverse books may be ordered through booksellers or by contacting:

iUniverse
1663 Liberty Drive
Bloomington, IN 47403
www.iuniverse.com
1-800-Authors (1-800-288-4677)

Because of the dynamic nature of the Internet, any Web addresses or links contained in this book may have changed since publication and may no longer be valid. The views expressed in this work are solely those of the author and do not necessarily reflect the views of the publisher, and the publisher hereby disclaims any responsibility for them.

ISBN: 978-1-4401-9454-2 (sc)
ISBN: 978-1-4401-9860-1 (ebook)

Printed in the United States of America

iUniverse rev. date: 11/30/2009

INTRODUCTION

This book is written by me, Evangelist Raymond K. Huff, who has been anointed by God to write poetry, based off the bible, and events of life. This book unlike any other, will allow you to see the scriptures, and many life situations, through poetry, that is anointed, and divinely written.

God has also anointed me to preach and teach his gospel, in hopes of bringing people to a better quality of life, concerning their souls, their mindset, and a life of peace, love, family and friends.

I was inspired to write this book, not only to share the gift that God has given me, but to shed some light on scriptures, explain some of life's situations, and to give humor, peace, and creative impacting thoughts on other matters that may or may not relate to you directly.

I thank God for my mother Sylvia, my son Andre, and my entire family, friends, and church family, First Church of Deliverance Inc. of Camden, NJ, that has inspired me, encouraged me, and often gave me honest critique concerning many of the poems I have written.

This book is in no wise designed to offend, oppress, ridicule, or belittle any persons, or any situation a person may have encountered in life.

I hope this book is a blessing to all those who read, or hear the poems read aloud and that you are blessed, entertained, and inspired by its content. I also pray that God gets the Glory, for the gift he has put in me, to share with you.

Be Blessed,

Raymond K. Huff

Derived From: Psalm 61:2 From the end of the earth will I cry unto thee, when my heart is overwhelmed: lead me to the rock that is higher than I.

LIFTED UP

I am under so much pressure, that I don't know where to start,
I can not see a resolution, and its overwhelming my heart.
I know I shouldn't stress, I shouldn't worry or doubt,
But those are natural human emotions, when you can't figure
something out.

So my nerves are on edge, my mind has no peace,
I struggle throughout the day, and can't get a good night's sleep.
So unto the Lord I pray, unto the Lord I cry,
Then he places me upon a rock, a rock that's higher than I.

My faith has been elevated, with evidence I can not see,
My situation has not changed, but there is a change in me.
I am no longer stressing, I now have joyful peace,
Praise throughout the day, and finally a good night sleep.

My heart was overwhelmed, but there's joy within,
For Jesus is that rock, and he allowed me to stand on him.

Raymond K. Huff

Derived From: <u>1 Kings 3:25</u> And the king said, divide the living child in two, and give half to the one, and half to the other.

CUT JUDGMENT

To cut the baby, or not the cut the baby,
Judgment must be sliced down the middle,
To solve this puzzle, to resolve this riddle.

To cut the baby, or not cut the baby,
One must be wise and understand,
For the decision made, will affect the land.

To hear the same story, with two different views,
To reach the truth, but yet with no clues.

Righteous judgment and the conclusion of life,
Have been placed in my hand, right under this knife.

To cut the baby, or not cut the baby,
To make one cry, will make one laugh,
To give one whole, or to give two half.

To cut the baby, or not cut the baby,
To look into, one's heart and soul,
And find a truth, that remains untold.

Divide the baby, yells the one,
Please don't do it, cries the other,
Sacrifice, has rightly discerned,
Where's the truth, and who's the mother.

A righteous verdict has been rendered,
In the land is peace and safety,
For I have learned to cut thru judgment,
And never intended to cut the baby.

Raymond K. Huff

WHERE DOES LOVE START?

Where does love begin? Where does love really start?
Is it at first sight? In your mind, or in your heart?

I know a real good person, and we get along alright,
But they want to be more than friends, however
they're not my type.

I love our conversations, and I want them in my life,
I can see us as friends forever, but not as husband and wife.

Is real love truly blind? Or should I open my eyes and see,
That here is a wonderful person, that says their in love with me.

But there are no sparks for me, no butterflies, or intuition,
No singing in the shower, no dancing around the kitchen.

Love's just not of the heart, love also dwells in your head,
It's also a physical emotion, that's shared by lovers in bed.

So when I come home in the evening, I want
someone in my sight,
That sparks the emotions of love, and satisfies my flesh at night.

Someone I think is beautiful, both outward and within,
Someone I desire to have, as a lover and a friend.

Oh no, they are not ugly, they're pretty nice in fact,
And they are attracted to me, I'm just not attracted back.

Maybe you think I am shallow, who knows, maybe you're right,
But will I be truly happy, with someone who is not my type.

I know appearances change, and beauty is within the eye,
But love should be wrapped in truth, and not hidden behind a lie.

For you can change your mind, but no one controls their heart,
So if there is no attraction, tell me where does love really start?

Raymond K. Huff

I'M AN USHER, THAT'S RIGHT!

I love the church I attend, it's a special part of my life,
I love the work I do, I'm an usher that's right.
See you may not think it much, but we play an important part,
Before the service begins, the ushers are there from the start.
We're there straightened up, getting programs envelopes and
fans,
Giving people pleasant greetings, friendly hugs, and shaking
hands,
Oh yes, I do more, than stand there, looking good while wearing
my white,
I am a part of ministry, I'm an usher, that's right.

Now ushering bad kids, that's a whole another story,
But before I lose my cool, I just stop and give God the glory,
Cause I got to tell 'em stop running, and stop jumping on the
pews,
And they be messing up my gloves, and stepping on my shoes.
Sometimes I want to yell, but I have be polite,
And I have to show temperance, cause I'm an usher, that's right.

Ushers set the church personality, in unity we should all work,
For we often are the ones who determine, if a visitor comes back
to our church
For we deal with the saints and sinners, church folks, family and
friends,
And it aint always easy, now can I get a couple Amens
Cause some folks get in the spirit, and be kicking me in my leg,
And one person got real happy, and started hitting me in head,
And I started thinking to myself, is this job really worth it,
Cause I don't think that's the spirit, I think they hitting me on
purpose.
And yes I got angry, and my flesh wanted to fight,
But I held my peace, cause I'm and usher, that's right.

Now I'm not the very first usher, If you think I was, I beg your
pardon,
See the Lord God was the first, When he ushered Adam and Eve
up out the Garden.
But ever since then, ushering had a purpose,
To be a part of ministry, in each and every service.
For when you deal with God's people, you have to do it with love
And be wise as a serpent, but yet gentle as a dove.
So I must pray for the right spirit, before I take my post,
And to be a real good usher, you need the Holy Ghost.

Because ushers don't miss a thing, we see it all, like it's our
mission,
From the opening hymn, until the benediction.
We will lead you to your seat, or greet you at the door,
And create an atmosphere, of peace and not of war.
We will march with the offerings, sing along with choir,
Encourage the preacher, and call the devil a liar.
See I do more than just stand there looking good wearing white,
I thank God I am an usher, an usher that's right!

Raymond K. Huff

THE EARTH IS THE LORD'S...

Derived From: <u>Genesis Chapter 7</u>
and Luke 17:27
They did eat, they drank, they married wives, they were given in marriage, until the day that Noah entered into the ark, and the flood came, and destroyed them all.

PREACHER MAN

Preacher man, preacher man, going around preaching everyday,
Telling everybody, that God's gonna make it rain.
Well you ain't gotta preach to me, oh no, just pass me by,
Cause how it's gonna rain, and ain't a cloud up in the sky.

Preacher man, preacher man, what's all that wood there for,
Said God told you to build an ark, with a window and a door.
And to get all the animals, line them up two by two,
And put them ark, so they can be safe with you.

Preacher man, preacher man, you should stop and think,
With all those animals in there, you know it's gonna stink,
And who in their right mind, would go anywhere,
In that silly looking thing, with a lion and a bear.

Preacher man preacher man, now that's a funny looking boat,
And even if it rained, that thing ain't gonna float.
Yall hear the preacher man, said God's been talking to him,
Well if God can make it rain, why can't God teach him to swim.

Oh preacher man, preacher man, I think you're insane,
What's that water hitting my head, oh my, it's starting to rain.
And look it keeps on raining, water done covered the land,
Maybe we should have listened to that old preacher man.

I know, I know, I shouldn't have hardened my heart,
And now it seems too late, to come into the ark?
Maybe you should listen, when someone is preaching,
It's gonna RAIN.

Raymond K. Huff

THOUGHTS OF YOU

When I Ponder over my past,
And think my whole life thru,
A smile comes over my face,
Whenever I think of you.

Some days I have the answers,
Some days not a clue,
But there's no mystery to solve,
When it comes to my thoughts of you

The glitter of stars at night,
The freshness of morning dew,
Is like heaven touching the earth,
And my mind is touching you.

As you see I have been thinking,
For this I often do,
And the best thoughts that I have,
Is how God blessed me with you.

Thank you for being a part of my life.

Raymond K. Huff

Derived From: Matthew 16:26 For what is a man profited, if he shall gain the whole world, and lose his own soul? Or what shall a man give in exchange for his soul?

WHAT COUNTS

If my life is the sum, of the things that I have,
Subtracted by my soul, going down a wayward path,
Then I'm divided into nothing, but you can do the math,
And then add up what really counts.

If I end up being famous, and shining like a star,
And traveled the world abroad, both near and far,
But my purpose here on earth, was bottled in a jar,
Then what is sealed, is what really counts.

Yes I want to prosper, and be in good health,
Live a long life, and obtain lots of wealth,
But I must remember, after this there's something else,
Because what I can take with me matters most.

For gold is not measured by pound, but the ounce,
So be careful what you value, and also what you trounce,
For the words "Well done", I want to hear God announce,
Then my life was worth living, and that's what really counts.

Raymond K Huff

Derived from <u>Psalm 91:1</u> He that dwelleth in the secret place of the most High shall abide under the shadow of the Almighty.

HIDE ME

Sometimes I feel, life's an ongoing test,
To the point where I feel, I am carrying too much stress.
The days are too short, I'm stretched to the limit,
I can't take another hour, but hold up wait a minute.
Because if explode, and lose my mind one day,
Folks will just talk, and you know what they'll say.
He use to be saved, and doing so very well,
But the devil got in him, and now he's full of hell.
But no one sees my troubles, my pains and tribulations.
And no one hears my cries, and my need for restoration.

I go to church its still there, I go to work its still there,
I talk to people its still there, and I don't really think they care
I read the bible its still there, go to revival its still there,
I then pray buts its still there, night and day its still there.

Lord hide me, Lord hide me, Lord hide me, Lord hide,
Because I just can deal, with all of this inside me.
I hear thunder, but God's not in it, I hear fire, Gods' not in it,
I hear lightning, God's not in it. but a little small voice.

And I hear God say...
Come unto me, you look burdened and heavy laden
I have been watching you, and hearing while your praying.
Take my yoke upon you, and then learn of me,
Your mind will be enlightened, and then your eyes will see.
That the burdens you been carrying I know you could bear,
So please stop being selfish, and like no one seems to care.

So he took me to a secret place, and there I did dwell,
To escape the agony that I felt, the torment and the hell.
It was there I found peace, unspeakable joy and rest,
It was there I became revived, renewed and refreshed.
And yes I learned patience, and temperance and love,
And stop looking towards man for help, and start looking up
above
And now I'm feeling good, strengthened and rightly,
For now I am walking, under, the shadow of the almighty.
And this new feeling I have, I think I'm gonna keep it,
Where's this place you ask? Well, it's a secret.

Raymond K. Huff

I PUT BEFORE YOU AN OPEN DOOR
THAT NO MAN CAN SHUT..

Derived From: <u>Luke 24:6</u>
He is not here, but is risen: remember how he spake unto you when he was yet in Galilee,

HE AIN'T THERE

Looking for Jesus that was crucified,
Who gave up the Ghost, hung his head and died?
Well he ain't there, he ain't there.

Looking for the Christ, whose flesh they did beat
Who still has nails in his hands and feet?
Well he ain't there, he ain't there
Stop looking in the grave, cause he ain't there.

Looking for Jesus, who is bloody red,
Mocked with a crown of thorns in his head?
Guess what? He ain't there!

You thought he'd still be there I suppose,
Lying in a tomb wrapped in grave clothes?
What did you come to the tomb to see?
Count your days, one two three,
And he told you he wouldn't be there.

He has risen, he defeated death,
He once was here, but he won then left,
So go testify, and tell the rest,
Jesus Christ is alive! Jesus is alive!
You didn't think he would rise?
Overcome death then ascend thru the skies?
But don't stand there just looking up

Look inside of you, examine your heart,
Ask him to come in, and take the center part,
Give him your soul, body, and mind
Truly seek the Lord, and you will surely find.

You will know the Lord, is faithful and true,
And wants to reside, in side of you,
Your life he will guide, your soul he will save,
And that's why he couldn't stay in the grave.

So don't look for Jesus in a cemetery,
He ain't there he ain't there!

Raymond K. Huff

Derived From: <u>1 Peter 5:2:</u> Care for the flock that God has entrusted to you. Watch over it willingly, not grudgingly—not for what you will get out of it, but because you are eager to serve God. (NLT)

PULPIT PIMP

Standing in the pulpit wearing your robe,
Reaching out to millions, all around the globe,
Or at your local church, with your priestly collar,
Looking for love, and the all mighty dollar.

You have come too far, you have been thru much,
To now go astray, and somehow lose touch,
So why live a life, that straddles the fence,
Why have you become a pulpit pimp?

You now have become, what you preached against,
An adulterer, a beggar, a pulpit pimp.

You should live to preach, and not preach to live
And put down others, that don't have to give,
And tell people things, like God will give it back,
While I am getting thin, your pockets getting fat.

Yea I know the church, needs money to survive,
That's why I give offerings, and pay my tithes,
But giving dollars to you, don't make sense,
You're an anointed con-man, a pulpit pimp

Yea, you can preach, and also prophesy,
But why teach the truth, and then live a lie,
Begging and begging, like you need more money,
But you are the joke, and the joke ain't funny.

Because when God gets ready, to let go his wrath,
Let's hear the joke, let's hear you laugh.
Cause you make hard for those who are true,
By the games that you play, and things that you do.

Manipulating women, and lying to the rest,
Cause your greedy for the money, and weak in your flesh,
But I write this poem, in hopes you will repent,
And get delivered from being, a pulpit pimp!

Raymond K. Huff

Derived from: Luke 11:35 Take heed therefore that the light which is in thee be not darkness.

THE TRUTH ABOUT ME

Does everyone lie? Or has everyone lied?
Does everyone have a place, where they can run and hide?
A place of solitude, that no one else can find,
A secret within your soul, a place within your mind.

Where you can be what you want, and say what ever you like,
And there is no one to judge you, or tell that's not right.
But thru my eyes only, the world I will see,
And I and only I, will know the truth about me

Not that I'm ashamed, or can't deal with the truth,
But some things will remain, housed under my roof.
Where the doors remained locked, and the lie is never free,
And I search every room, to learn the truth of me.

Am I good or evil? Should I be sad and shame?
Should I repent for my secrets? Or is someone else to blame?
Was it part of my destiny, or did I error with my soul?
Did I choose the wrong path, or was it out of my control?

Am I dreaming the truth? Or am I living a lie?
Should I wake up and see, there is no reason why.
There are no blueprints of life, no direction we must take,
Just live day by day, with every step we make.

For God gives us choices, so I must understand,
That storms may change my image, like the water does the sand.
But the sand is still sand, even when the castle fades,
So I will live with myself, and the choices that I have made.

I will not live under guilt, that others think I should have,
I will grow as I go, and learn from every path.
I will go within my soul, and set the lies free,
I will know who I am, and the truth about me.

Raymond K. Huff

Derived From: 1 Corinthians 6:20 For ye are bought with a price: therefore glorify God in your body, and in your spirit, which are God's.

ITS PRICELESS

What God has done for me is Priceless,
How he set me free is Priceless,
I am unable to repay, so I lift my hands and say,
Lord thank you,
For paying the price for me.

For God to have me in his plan is Priceless
And snatch from the devils hand, is Priceless,
I give God thanks every day,
Weather skies are blue or gray,
Thank God for paying the price for me.

When I pray, and he hears it, is Priceless,
To fill me with the Holy Spirit is Priceless
Lord do what you may, and your word I will obey,
For you alone paid the price for me

To die on Calvary Cross, Is Priceless
To save me when I was lost, is Priceless
To take nails in his hand, for the sins of every man
Dear Lord, I sincerely thank you, for the price for me.

Raymond K. Huff

FIRST LADY INDEED

I remember the time, I remember the year,
I was sitting in a pew, right over there,
When this woman walked in, beaming like the sun,
And Pastor started yelling, My Lord she's the one!

He pounded his chest, didn't hesitate or tarry,
But told everyone, she's the one I'm gonna marry.
Now I must admit, just like he said,
About eight months later, the two of them wed,
But that didn't make her our first lady.

See to be a first lady, you must be heaven sent,
Not just the wife of a Pastor, or some President,
But sent by God, with a particular plan,
To a particular place, with a particular man

See some ladies, are ladies in greed,
Or ladies in need, who should take heed,
Often mislead, and cannot succeed,
Not anointed nor appointed, to hold such a creed.
But our first lady, is a first lady indeed.

When she came in she prayed with us,
Joined the church and stayed with us,
She earned our love, respect and trust.
You could see that God, was making her.

Now some come in, and disrespect,
And change the title to lady elect,
Yea I know you read the book of John
He wrote elect lady, and that's just fine.
But in this case, there was no election,
No other woman, no other selection,

No crooked angles, no third dimension
The title is First Lady, No others to mention!

Now back to my poem.

Everything she does is under a scope,
For she sits in a place to give other women hope,
Of how to be a mother, and how to be a spouse,
How to be a wise woman, who knows how to build her house.

How to be a sister, and how to be a friend,
How to sit above, but yet fit in.
How to raise her children, how to act at work,
How to deal with women around her husband,
Cause he's the Pastor of the church.
Oh it really takes God to make her.

I will conclude this poem at Proverbs 31,
This virtuous woman, who still beams like the sun,
Who sent by God to be the Pastor's wife,
To do him good not evil, all the days of his life.
Who can find a virtuous woman?
That's been the question for years,
But the answer to that? My Pastor did.

And she is our First Lady,
First Lady Indeed!

Raymond K. Huff

(Dedicated to First Lady Yvonne Moorefield)

Derived From: 2 Peter 1:3
His divine power has given us everything we need for life and godliness through our knowledge of him who called us by his own glory and goodness. (NIV)

BE AWARE

Be mindful; be aware, smart and wisely guided,
Stop, look and listen, see what God's provided.

There are things in your midst, to bless your fellow man
But you must open your mind, be aware and understand.

You have purpose here on earth, but there are steps you have to take,
You can live out your dreams, and even be awake.

So arise this very day, with the a mindset to achieve,
And don't doubt, or look down, but look up and believe.

Take advantage of opportunity; don't let it pass you by,
For the only way to fail, is if you fail to try.

For God has kept you today, for something nice and new,
So be aware of the tools, that he's provided for you.

Raymond K. Huff

ENDURE YOUR JOURNEY

Derived From: <u>Mathew 27:3</u>
Then Judas, which had betrayed him, when he saw that he was condemned, repented himself, and brought again the thirty pieces of silver to the chief priests and elders,

WHAT DID I JUST DO

I walked with the man, I ate with the man,
I knew who the man was, but yet, what did I just do?
To a man who called me friend, to a man who cleansed my sin
Did I just betray him, or what did I just do?

I seen him feed the hungry, I seen him raise the dead,
And now I am the reason, those thorns are in his head.
Was it I or the devil that did that to the Christ?

Should I feel bad, after all he has power,
And was it my fault, or was it just his hour?
Maybe I can blame time, maybe I can hide my guilt.
But if it wasn't my fault, why am I torn apart,
Why at that last supper did the devil enter my heart?
After all it was twelve of us there,

Why did they choose me, to hold the moneybag?
Why didn't they rebuke me, and not care if I got mad?
Why did the prophets speak of me, in years of old?
Couldn't someone warn me, that the greatest story told,
Would end up with me doing what I just I did?

For 30 pieces of silver, and a kiss on the cheek,
Was all that was needed for such wickedness and deceit?
But I gave the money back, and I tried to avoid the plan,
But now I stand here guilty, with this rope in my hand.
I can't believe I am about to do this.

But how can a man live who betrays the Christ,
How can a man die, when he has given others life.
So now my body is hanging, there's no life inside of me,
And cursed is every man, that hangs from a tree,

Judas Iscariot, this is your life,
To be remembered forever, as the man who betrayed Christ,
For if evil enters your heart, and that evil you do not rid,
You may betray the Lord, then wonder what you just did.

Raymond K. Huff

This poem is written for all those who loved someone,
but they didn't love you back.

LOVE ME BACK?... NO

Oh for so long, and for so many years,
My love for you was strong, and over came all fears,
But did you love me back? (pause) No.

Whenever you called I came, and offered you my help,
Often enduring shame, I induced upon myself.
But did you love me back? (pause) No.

You accepted all of me, and you knew how I felt,
It was so hard to see, you with someone else,
And wondering why you couldn't love me like that

Being rejected and torn apart, is a hard pill to swallow,
I tried to turn my heart, but where you went it followed,
With hopes one day you would love me back

You love me, but you're not in love? But yet want me as a friend?
My mind can grasp this thought, but my heart can't comprehend.
My friends say it's not worth it, and I should let you be,
But I thought we were perfect, but loving eyes still can't see.

And since you wasn't cruel to me, it was so hard to leave,
But yet you made a fool of me, for never did you believe,
That we would share endless love, and like a flower in the sun
we'd grow,
And did you ever really love me back?
The painful truth is no.

Written with tears,
Raymond K. Huff

LOVE ME BACK

Derived from: <u>Galatians 5:17</u> For the flesh sets its desire against the Spirit, and the Spirit against the flesh; for these are in opposition to one another, so that you may not do the things that you please. (NASB)

THE LIFETIME WAR

From the day that I was born, and took my very first breath,
I was in the middle of a war, my spirit against my flesh.
See, I was formed to praise God, but yet born in sin,
And there started the conflict, going on deep within.

My flesh has desires, for pleasure, lust, and fun,
Knowing one day I would die, and this life will be done.
My flesh wants to tell lies, wants drugs, liquor and sex,
It wants, what it wants, and doesn't give a damn what happens next.

But my spirit wants the Lord, his peace and liberty,
Looking beyond this earthly time, and thinking eternity.
My spirit says resist, the temptations, and every lie,
Knowing that the soul that sins, it shall surely die.

Ever day is a struggle, from the moment that I arise,
And strength is awarded, thru my ears, and thru my eyes,
What I hear or what I see, all of the day long,
Determines if my flesh or my spirit will grow strong.

So my flesh seeks a path, my spirit hopes not to find,
For whoever wins the war, gains control of my mind.
So my thoughts are now involved, as is my soul,
What a mighty war, for conquer and control.

They fight for my dreams, while I am asleep,
My flesh loves the nightmares, my spirit loves the peace.
So I seek the Word of God, to give strength to my spirit,
But flesh gets irritated, and doesn't want to hear it.

But I make my flesh submit, and I refrain from sin,
But some days I am weak, and the flesh starts to win.
So I repent to the Lord, and ask him for help,
To do the things I need to do, but can not do by myself.

Lord please give me strength, so I may do what's right,
And overcome all evil, and live a peaceful life.
But I've lived in the flesh, since the day I was born,
But I walk in the spirit, therefore the war goes on.

Raymond K Huff

THANK YOU FOR TODAY

If I never see your smile again,
If you are never with me,
If I never see your lovely face,
Then thanks for the memory.

But I don't want to leave here,
Not saying what I have to say,
I don't want to wait till tomorrow,
I'd rather tell you today.
Thank you for the laughter,
The good times and the fun,
Thank you for today, if tomorrow never comes.

And if I never place your hands in mine,
If our time has reached eternity,
If I never hold you close to me again,
Then thanks for the memory.

To be with you always, is what I often pray,
But if I am denied, thank you for today.
Thank you for the talks
And all the things you've done
Thank you for today, if tomorrow never comes.

Give God thanks, is what I want to do,
For I was glad that I was able to share
Some of my life with you.

For when this life is over, there is nothing left to say,
So I love you, and thank you for today.
I really love you, and thank you for today.

Raymond K. Huff
(Dedicated to my dear friend Tummona Fisher)

GOD KNOWS WHAT'S BEST

Some days I just wonder, some nights I haven't slept,
Of a time not fulfilled, of a promise that wasn't kept.
For I thought years was promised, that we would share the same
ground,
I never had a dream, where you were not around.

I thought we'd grow old together, eat, joke, and laugh,
Talk about the days of old, and things of the past.
The past came to the present, and took me by surprise,
And now, how can I laugh, with so many tears in my eyes.

For I felt that God had failed me, I felt he did me wrong,
And you left me far to soon, and wasn't here that long
I needed to place my blame, but God makes no mistakes,
For this life is measured by time, but he has an eternal place.

I will always think of you, but it's still hard to accept,
That our time wasn't fulfilled, and promises wasn't kept.
But in peace I will live, and in peace you will rest,
And I will keep my faith in God, for God knows what is best.

Raymond K. Huff

(Dedicated to my nephew Eddie,
and all those who lost loved ones at an early age)

Derived From: 1 Thessalonians 5:18 In every thing give thanks: for this is the will of God in Christ Jesus concerning you

GIVE THANKS

So many things going on, so many things seem so wrong,
I want to make a joyful noise, but I hear a sad song.
The bad news, the tragedies, the sorrows, the pains,
And the windows of my heart, is pounded by the rains.

For everyone can see, the world from a different view,
But the greatest sight of all is God's sight of you.
Does he see you happy? Does he see you grin?
Or has the evil of this world, darkened your spirit within?

Have you lost the ability, to see from a different side?
Can you still raise your hands, and shout "Thank you dear God?"
Can you be thankful for today, and dream about tomorrow?
Or will you live your life in misery, and drown in tears of sorrow?

The first sign of happiness, is to know that it exist,
The next thing you should do, is always remember this,
No matter where you go, or what others do,
Give thanks unto the Lord; it's his will concerning you.

Raymond K. Huff

Derived From: <u>1 Samuel 16:10</u> Again, Jesse made seven of his sons to pass before Samuel. And Samuel said unto Jesse, The LORD hath not chosen these. 11 And Samuel said unto Jesse, Are here all thy children? And he said, There remaineth yet the youngest, and, behold, he keepeth the sheep. And Samuel said unto Jesse, Send and fetch him: for we will not sit down till he come hither.

THEY DIDN'T INVITE ME

The prophet comes to town, to anoint a king, and comes
to my house,
My dad calls my brothers, they all get in line
But me? I am left out.

My brothers walk past the prophet, they all walk back and forth,
They all anxiously await, for the prophet to pour the oil.

My oldest brother is tall and handsome, He could surely play the
part,
The prophet thinks it's him, he is ready pour the oil
But God has seen his heart,

He refused all my brothers, not one of them pass,
And never did they guess,
To say hold on, where's David?
Hold up, there's one left,
Oh no, they didn't invite me.

But the prophet says to my dad, there must be another son,
My father then remembers, and says yes there is one,
I was out back with the sheep, never called to the front,
Writing poems like the Lord's my Shepherd, and I shall not want.

But I finally got my invitation, so I came on in,
The prophet hears from heaven, and shouts out
Yes! That's him!

So the prophet pours the oil, anointed me the next king,
Right in front for my brothers to see,
So even though I wasn't invited, the party was still for me.

You didn't get your invitation either, Here's what you do my
friend
Keep worshipping God, until they invite you in.
And then God will speak, He will not hid his voice
And they will know who is anointed, because they won't have
a choice

Raymond K. Huff

Derived from: Matthew 27:42 He saved others; himself he cannot save. If he be the King of Israel, let him now come down from the cross, and we will believe him.

KEEP LOOKING, KEEP LOOKING

People looking at me, wondering what I'm gonna do,
Wondering within themselves, if my salvation is true,
Think they know what's going on, but really don't have a clue,
But keep looking, God is going to save me,
Keep looking.

People thinking, how did I get in this mess,
And how can I suffer and still say I am blessed,
And will I keep my integrity, as I go thru this test,
Well keep looking, God is going to save me,
Keep looking.

They make hard statements, that cut me like a knife,
And wonder if I really got the spirit of Christ,
But God is about to do, something wonderful in my life,
So stay tuned, and keep looking,

I may be in a wilderness, but please note, I ain't loss,
For my destiny demands, that I bear a heavy cross,
For I know who I am, and to whom I belong,
And I got a feeling, things are about to change,

Trouble don't last all ways, Trouble don't last all ways,
So in advance I worship, and give God the Praise,
I may be in a mess right now, but in a couple more days,
God is going to save me, and God is going to raise me,
So please keep looking, just keep on looking.

Raymond K. Huff

MY BRAIN IS FRIED

So many thoughts going thru my head, where my soul is
searching for peace
My body yearns for a pillow, and looks forward to a good night
sleep.

With so much going on at work, and at home with every day stress,
My thoughts are mentally fatigued, and my brain needs to take a
deep breath.

As I try to gather my thoughts, and hold one at a time,
And search for that place of solitude that I know exist in my mind.

A place where there is no drama and everything appears as it seems,
And I don't have to be asleep, and still visualize my dreams.

I can handle what I have to, and nothing is overly wrong,
But sometimes twenty-four hours, seems to take so long.
I don't want to hurry life, but yet I don't want to wait,
I just need to clear my head, I need a change of fate.

No one can live my life for me, no one can know how I really feel,
My words only share a portion, of what my mind has to conceal.

For if my mind had a voice, it would speak louder than my mouth
And all that's in my brain would simultaneously come out.

It would come out like a river, and overflow like storm
And the flood my environment, with everything that's going on.

But some words I can not speak, even when tempted or tried
I just boil within myself, and that's why my brain is fried.

Raymond K. Huff

2 Timothy 2:20 But in a great house there are not only vessels of gold and of silver, but also of wood and of earth; and some to honour, and some to dishonour. 21 If a man therefore purge himself from these, he shall be a vessel unto honour, sanctified, and meet for the master's use, and prepared unto every good work.

VESSEL OF HONOR

When God has a plan, that he wants to accomplish on earth,
He sanctifies a man, and anoints him prior to birth.
He gives that man wisdom, understanding, temperance and love,
And his life becomes a testimony, to give glory to the Father
above.

So down in Rayne, Louisiana, on January twenty second,
God began a work, back in 1912 I reckon.
When Bishop Curly Guidry, had began to be,
Prepared for the master's use, prepared for his journey.

A journey that would lead him, to have Mother Miriam as his wife,
Where they would serve the Lord in holiness, at the Church of
God in Christ.
So we thank God for what he's done, where he's going and where
he's been,
For he is a vessel of honor, and we thank God for him.

We can talk about all the money, that has been raised,
The dues that's been paid, the things that have been made,
All the escapades, and wonderful accolades,
But if God wasn't in it, it would just be a parade.
But this is not a parade, it's a wonderful, holy story,
A testimony of greatness, whereby we give God glory.

Now we know that he isn't God, so we don't need to hear from
debaters,
But he is a man of God, so run tell that to all the haters.

Cause every time I dig a well, someone's there with a shovel,
But tonight we're happy in Jesus, and ain't nobody mad but the
devil

So we should all be happy, about whom God has raised,
It's marvelous in our eyes, and for this we give God praise.
And to give honor to a man, oh no, it's not a sin,
We're not thanking him for God, but we're thanking God for
him.

We appreciate his service, his works in many fields,
We appreciate this church, which God led him to build,
We appreciate the Word, that God speaks thru his mouth,
We appreciate his power, to rebuke the devil out.
We appreciate his prayers, and his hands that God has used,
We appreciate his members, that fill up the pews,

Thank God for all he's done, thank God for everything,
In Glassboro, NJ, right here at Healing Wings.
It isn't easy leading God's people, dealing with saints, sinners and
friends,
And I wish I had a witness, that would give me a couple amen's.
For God used Abraham, to produce in his ninety's its true,
But Bishop Guidry is still producing, you don't believe, me look
at you.

So tonight let's get excited, about this man whom God has called,
Let's get up on our feet, let's get ready to applause.
For this great Man of God, who has stood thru thick and thin,
Bishop Guidry a vessel of honor, we thank God for him.
A vessel of honor, and we thank God for him!

Evangelist Raymond K. Huff

TUG OF LOVE

Love shouldn't hurt, it shouldn't leave you sore
It shouldn't be a tug of love; it shouldn't be a tug of war.

A man should not hit a woman, try to bring her harm,
Then think the words I'm sorry, will lead her back into his arms.
And a woman shouldn't provoke a man, call him hurtful names,
Then think he will stand there, and not retaliate the pain.

Love shouldn't put me down, and leave me hurting on the floor,
It just shouldn't be a tug of love; it shouldn't be a tug of war.

A man shouldn't use money, to buy love and affection,
And try to lead the way, but yet has no direction.
A woman shouldn't use her body, to obtain money and gifts,
And not realize the day will come, when she'll have nothing to
buy with.

Love shouldn't have a price tag; love shouldn't be a retail store.
You can not pay for love, for money won't end the war.

Yes love will cost you something, and both must pay their part,
But together love is fulfilled, when it's paid from the heart.

So love should bring you home, it tells where to be,
For one plus one is still two, and love does not include three.
So don't tell me that you love, but yet abuse my trust,
For real love is compromise, that changes all of us

So show me who you are, show me the character within,
And I will see if I can love you, but then and only then.
For I refuse to travel the road, where my heart is hurt to the core,
I refuse to play tug of love, for love should not be a war.

Raymond K. Huff

BIRDS HAVE NEST

Derived from: John 21:16 He saith to him again the second time, Simon, son of Jonas, lovest thou me? He saith unto him, Yea, Lord; thou knowest that I love thee. He saith unto him, Feed my sheep.

DO WE LOVE HIM?

How do you know if you love God,
Are the words I love you, just something to say?
How can we show how much we love him?
If we choose not to obey?

If you love him, then you must trust him,
And you will follow wherever he leads,
For God is love, and love is God,
And his sheep, you should feed.

The sheep are his people, not perfect at all,
And they come in all sought of colors,
But loving God can only be seen,
By the way we love each other.

Black, yellow, red and white,
The spirit of man is not based on race,
For love can not see the color of skin,
But is color blind, like God's loving grace.

So if we love God, we will keep his commandments,
We will trust in his word, and do what he say,
For if God asked you to feed sheep,
Would you look at their color, or would you obey?

Raymond K. Huff

MY BLACK BUTTERFLY

She flew into my life, when I was not expecting a thing,
But with such elegance and beauty, which rested upon her wing.
She stopped, hesitated, and then began to speak,
And at that very moment, I noticed something unique.
I could not vocalize it, but watched as she flew by,
This pleasant beautiful woman, this beautiful black butterfly.

I listen to every word, as she spoke into the air,
I was cultivated by her beauty, and tried hard not to stare.
But this woman was like an angel, a special gift is she,
I was blessed that very day, that she landed next to me.

Her presence is a flow of Godliness, seasoned with his grace,
With a heavenly glow upon her, that's shone upon her face.
A heart of love and mercy, a spirit of joy and cheer,
She is a conqueror of peace, and over comer of fear.
She walks upon the earth, lifting the spirits of others high,
She spreads her wings of love, my beautiful black butterfly.

She's endured the waves of life, like the waters upon the shore,
She seeks a path of peace, she a lover of what is pure.
To look upon her beauty, or to have her in your view,
Your mind could not imagine, the trials that she's been thru.
Life's evils clipped her wings, but thru God she's been restored,
Now she delivers to others, the salvation of the Lord.

There is a healing in her story, where victory has been earned.
How she survived the floods and fires, and has not been drowned
nor burned.

Patience has become her sister, comfort is child,
Strength is in her touch, and encouragement in her smile.
For the glory of God is upon her, and it's seen in her eye,
She's my dear and lovely friend, my beautiful black butterfly.
I am for you, as you are for I,
Never be caged again, my beautiful black butterfly.

Raymond K. Huff

(Dedicated to my friend, Denise Conyers)

MY BEAUTIFUL BLACK BUTTERFLY

Derived From: <u>Job 1:8</u> And the LORD said unto Satan, Hast thou considered my servant Job, that there is none like him in the earth, a perfect and an upright man, one that feareth God, and hates evil?

HAVE YOU CONSIDERED?

The devil wanted to prove, that men are just all talk,
So in and out the earth he began to walk.
He's not seeking church goers, nor people that's seeking power,
But seeking those who love God, seeking whom he may devour.
So he dares to approach God, and tells God of his plan,
And God says have you considered, Job, a righteous man?

Have you considered him?

The devil really believes, that if God lets him try,
He could make Job lose faith; make him curse God and die.
So God removes his hedge, and watches from above,
As the devil tries to prove, what does Job really love?
So he takes Job's possessions, and now Job is broke,
He loses all that he has, but Job still has hope.

His friends seem to mock him, his wife leaves his side,
He is sick unto death, but still won't curse God.
So many prayers and questions, relish thru his mind,
But yet he has patience, and waits on his appointed time.
Oh what a price to pay, Oh, what a hefty toll,
But what will a man give, in exchange for his soul

You can't love God for things, Or to get that and this,
But true love for God, Is to love him for who he is.
So when everything is going wrong, and you don't understand why
Will you be able to stand, or will you curse God and die?

Job passed his test, and everything was restored,
Job kept his integrity, and now he is overjoyed,
Yes he was angry, yes he did fuss,
And even though God had sleighed him
In God did he trust.

So the question I now ask, is what would you do?
Or even better yet, would God consider you?
Hmmm Would God consider you?

Raymond K. Huff

Derived From: Genesis 25:30 &33 And Esau said to Jacob, Feed me, I pray thee, with that same red pottage; for I am faint: therefore was his name called Edom. ³³And Jacob said, Swear to me this day; and he sware unto him: and he sold his birthright unto Jacob.

THE DEALER AND THE ADDICT

Jacob had a substance; Esau had to have it,
Jacob was the dealer, and Esau was the addict.

The desire for a substance, changed his course of life,
Sorrow became his sister, misery became his wife.

He had a special purpose, from the day of his birth,
But now that has changed, as he crawls upon the earth.

His actions has changed his name, a lie became his truth,
And now lives are lost, because of substance abuse.

For Jacob had a substance, and Esau had to have it,
Jacob was the dealer, and Esau was the addict.

No one ever believes, how their life will now change,
No one ever sees, the years of ongoing pain.

The second you partake, is the minute you are hooked,
And the hours become days, before you get a second look.

Being trapped with desire, for something that can kill,
Is a hard battle to fight, a strong matter of will.

Some say it's a sickness, some say a disease,
That paralyzes nations, and brings the mighty to their knees,

Some say it's a weakness, some say it's a sin,
A deal with the devil, that you allow to come in.

For some it has led to prison, some to their grave,
Is there any help? For only God can save.

But Jacob still had a substance, and Esau still had to have it,
Jacob was his dealer and Esau was his addict.

Do you see who you are, and know what you've become,
Can you feel your pain, or are you now numb?

Can you escape your darkness, can you leave your jail,
Your wall without windows, your prison without a cell.

Can you somehow get back, the years of yesterday?
Can you find your birthright, the one you threw away?

Can you feel the prayers of loved ones, can you feel how they
hurt,
Does medicine make you better? And does rehab really work?

Should we be blame the addict, or the dealer who provides,
Or should we curse them all, or let the Lord decide.

For this are not just words, gathered in a poem,
But its love and it is pain, that has hit every home.

For I have seen lives changed, I've seen homes destroyed,
I have seen kids grow up, feeling lost and feeling void.

I have seen fathers give up hope; I've seen mothers with teary
eyes,
Wondering if their children can ever change their lives.

Praying a day will come, when they will find the truth,
For many have lost their way, on a path of drug abuse.

For Jacob had a substance, and Esau had to have it,
Jacob was the dealer, and Esau was the addict.

Raymond K. Huff

(Dedicated to all addicts, and praying for their deliverance)

Derived From: <u>Ecclesiastes 10:19</u> A feast is made for laughter, and wine maketh merry: but money answereth all things.

MONEY ANSWERS

So you have dreams, visions and needs,
People to cloth, and mouths to feed.
Pastoral Care and Church up keep,
Financial plans and task to complete,
Well Money Answers All Things!

I know you can't serve God and money too,
But here is a word for every pew,
How can the church ever survive?
If we only get money from the people inside?

The story of the three men with talents,
Was about money and economical balance,
Of how the people of God should grow,
How to invest and where to sow.
Well done my good and faithful servant

Although you get taxed, from where you are blessed,
You can truly be saved from I R S,
Learn financial investment and blessings it brings,
And then let your money answer more things.

The church can sing, dance and pray,
But after benediction its time to pay,
Pay for you dreams, visions, and task,
And here is the answer before you can ask.
Money Answer All Things!

Raymond K. Huff

53

A FAMILY THAT PRAYS TOGETHER...

I WANNA CRY

I wanna cry, there is nothing wrong, so don't ask me why,
But I know that I know, I just wanna cry.
Sometimes I need to cry, I need time to unfold,
I need to shed a tear, and purify my soul.

I heard that crying is like taking your soul to the laundry matt,
Sanctify me, wash me clean, then allow me time to dry,
Refreshed I will be, stained and dirt free, as I began to cry.

Sometimes I'm all alone, contemplating about life,
Thinking about my struggles, my miscrics and strife.
I also think of accomplishments, and wonderful people I know
And the complexity of thoughts, causes tears to flow.
Some say you shouldn't cry, but no one ever said why,
Just a tear or two, not a long boo hoo, But it could be good to cry.

Sometimes I hear a song, and it takes me to a time,
When life was fulfilled, dreams became real, and I had peace of
mind.
Then I start to think, how that moment slipped away,
Tears began to fall, for the thoughts of yesterday.
And how I want to go back, and relive those days and then,
I think about the loss, of family members and friends.

I'm not too friendly with death, though it's a part of being born
But time belongs to no one, therefore time goes on.
And the sunshine of today, can not change my yester years,
Can not change my painful past, can not hold back my tears.
But I will not live in my past, but will heal from every sore,
Whether my fault or not, for it, I cry no more.
But now I shed tears, for the whole world to see,
Tears of joy and gladness, that God's been good to me.
So don't focus on my tears, in them no story is told,

They are a mere reflection, of the fountain within my soul.
So now when I look back, and think about my past,
I may start to cry, and at the very same time I laugh.
I cry because I'm happy, I laugh because I'm free,
For the Lord still watches the sparrows, and he still watches me.

So at any given time, and at any given place,
I may start to smile, and have tears running down my face.
I just might want to cry, I might want to unfold,
I might want to shed a tear, and purify my soul.
I just might want to cry.

Raymond K. Huff

Derived From: 2 Timothy 4:7 I have fought a good fight,
I have finished my course, I have kept the Faith:
2 Timothy 3:14 But continue thou in the things which thou hast learned and hast been assured of, knowing of whom thou hast learned them;

WALK ON ME

I use to be a pillar, holding up the church,
Supporting Ministry, always finding work.
I helped where I could, I stood strong and tall,
Watching as well as praying, like a watchman on the wall.
I gave my time and money, I was faithful and bold,
To be a pillar in the church, where the Lord saved my soul.
I helped out where I could, in the back or in the front,
And the Lord did sustain me, there was no lack or want.

Now don't get me wrong, I haven't slid back nor down,
I'm still on my course, just a little older now.
And the young they are strong, the old know the way,
So in the same position, none are able to stay.
So as I get older, and peak towards life ridge,
I find myself transforming, from a pillar into a bridge.
So go ahead walk on me.

For as bridge I don't stand up, but I do carry across,
Those who may be weary, those who may be lost.
Those who have desire, to travel from shore to shore,
And establish a new foundation, where they've never been before.
I can carry you over valleys, and over cliffs so steep,
I can lead up to the heavens, or to mountain peaks,
Lead you over many dangers, where violence does abound,
And over troubled waters, I will gladly lay me down
I will be the bridge, that will help avoid a fall,
And carry you to a land, where others can only call.

57

And yes I'm still faithful, and yes I'm still bold,
So as you cross this bridge, make sure to pay your toll.
Pay me my respect, pay me what I'm due,
Pay me for sustaining, a work left for you.
Pay me with a thank you, for all the things I give,
Whether as a pillar, or this older and wiser bridge.
Please use my knowledge, my wisdom and my past,
To bridge the gaps of life, so that ministry will always last.
Learn from my mistakes, and all the things I did,
And when you get where ya going, Thank God for this Bridge.

Raymond K. Huff

YOUR OPINION OF ME?

I call you friend, and not my foe,
And some things, I want you to know,
Things of my the heart, and things in my mind,
That tears me apart, but helps me to shine.

I share with secrets with you, for I deeply feel,
That you will never hurt me, or make it a big deal,
This is the zest of my day, and the comfort of my night,
That I can share with you, my wrongs, and my right.

But I must tell you, I feel a little weird,
For sharing myself aloud, sometimes makes me scared.
Scared to open up, and share what's inside,
It's always been easier, to cover up and hide.

But with you I took the chance, to open up my life,
Like a surgery performed, but yet without a knife,
So if you're going to judge me, judge me with the truth,
And if you can't do that, sew me up, then cut me loose.

For I am who I am, and I won't be oppressed,
I won't pretend to be at peace, yet have a different address,
So take me as I am, for I am what you see,
Just promise to be honest, with your opinion of me.

Raymond K. Huff

LOVELY & DARK

I know a lady, who is dark and lovely,
She is Lovely and dark,
So this falls between,
My eyes and my heart.

She makes my heart pound,
Skip a beat or two,
And makes my eyes lather,
Whenever she's in view.

She's dark and lovely, Lovely and dark,
To the end of her beauty,
Right from the start.

Like a smooth flowing river,
Powerful but loose,
Like a soft black berry, and sweet like its juice

Her sexiness is clever, and appeals to the eye,
With a serenity of peace,
Like a calm midnight sky.

Skin touched by the sun,
And caressed by the moon,
She's a rhythm of pure beauty,
A soft melodious tune.

She is curvy and courageous,
Sensual and smart,
She's dark and she's lovely,
She is lovely and dark.

Live on, beautiful dark lady, live on!

Raymond K. Huff

Derived From: <u>2 Samuel 11:3</u> And David sent and enquired after the woman. And one said, Is not this Bathsheba, the daughter of Elim, the wife of Uriah the Hititite?

WHAT ABOUT ME?

I was taking a bath, my husband was at war,
Then my life changed, because what the king had saw.
Never did I know, I was in the king's view,
I had no idea, what he was plotting to do.

He summoned me, he wanted me, and I didn't have a choice,
For everyone had to obey, when you heard the kings voice.
He made me an adulterous, he made me sad and shame,
He made me a lowly woman, that he put under his name.

He tried to cover his sins, sent my husband to the front,
He impregnated me with child, and not ask me what I want.
I was in love with my husband, and glad to be his spouse,
And now I share a man, with several women in the house.

Oh how my life has changed, as I search for the truth,
On that day I took a bath, while the king was on the roof.

Now I am a widow, now my child is dead,
And there's one daunting question, that's still ringing in my head.
My name is Bathsheba and what about me?

Raymond K. Huff
(On behalf of Bathsheba)

LIKE A TREE PLANTED BY THE WATERS,
I SHALL NOT BE MOVED

Derived From: Jeremiah 10:19 Woe is me for my hurt! My wound is grievous; but I said, truly this is a grief, and I must bear it.

THE PURPOSE OF MY PAIN

Oh what pain I am in, the agony makes me cry,
But yet I carry a smile and people wonder why.
Wonder why I won't break down, is the thoughts throughout the crowd,
Yet they cannot hear my tears, for I refuse to cry out loud.

But I know my pain has a purpose.

Maybe God has allowed, this pain in my life,
To be a testimony, about the pains of Christ.
And how he did suffer, for things he did not do,
And maybe the pain I have, is meant to save a few.

For some things in happen in life, that no one is able to change,
So I've learned to carry my cross, I've learned to bear my pain.
And my smile is not fake, I'm happy as can be,
I will testify to others, that God's been good to me.

And If I never fully understand, this burden I must toll,
I'll have the peace of mind, that my God is in control.
He will comfort me in the sun, and shield me from the rain,
And he alone will define, the purpose of my pain.

Raymond K. Huff

SMOOTHER THAN THAT

There are many things that are smooth to the skin,
But none of those things can touch a person within.
And silk is the fabric, that comes to mind,
When I think of smooth, soft and refined
But your smoother than silk.

Gold is very precious, diamonds are quite rare,
But they don't tell the story, of what people share.
So I may have some silk, a diamond and some gold,
But what I value now, is truth being told.

Of how someone special, has become my friend,
Like Gold to my riches, like silk on my skin
And your value is still growing.

There are five senses that make up a man
So you have to be more, than a touch of the hand.
So smell then taste, listen and see,
And what I'm looking at is looking back at me.
And she is so so smooth.

But my senses only connect me, to material things,
Like soft silk sheets, gold and diamond rings.
But there are some things, materials can't intake,
Like the chemistry of us, and the magic that we make.

The rare essence of you, when you walk in the door,
The pleasing presence of you that I gracefully adore.
The thoughts I have of you, when you're not in my sight,
The peaceful dreams of you, that appear in the night.
Your strength and you courage, and how you demand respect,
The cuteness of your laughter, and your ability to protect.
A beautiful package you are, cute and nicely wrapped
You're smooth just like silk
NO!
Smoother than that.

Raymond K. Huff

MY LOVE DESIRES YOU NOW

As The Sun Shines In the Sky,
And The Earth Rotates Around,
You're the Star of My Life,
And My Love Desires You Now.

The Thoughts of You in My Arms,
The Memory of Your Kiss,
For The Second You Step Away,
Is The Moment You Are Missed.

So Wherever Love Remains,
My Heart Will Be Found,
For I Yearn To Be Where You Are,
And My Love Desires You Now.

The Sun Rules the Day,
Then Makes Room for the Moon to Shine,
So I Sleep and Dream of You,
And Awake With You On My Mind.

My Eyes Enjoy Your Beauty,
My Ears Lavish Your Sound,
My Hands Reach Out To Touch You,
And My Love Desires You Now.

Again I Say, My Love Desires You Now.

Raymond K. Huff

CHRISTMAS EVE & MY BIBLE

T'was the night before Christmas and all thru the house,
I started thinking to myself what was Christmas all about.
Church wasn't open, we wasn't having a revival,
So I sat in my chair and opened up my bible.
I read the book of Genesis and about God's creations,
And some prophecies told in the book of revelations.
I read the story of Adam and Eve,
And by talking to the serpent, they both got deceived.
I then read the story of how Cain killed Abel,
I said man this is better than some stuff on cable.

I read about the flood, and Noah's ark,
How it rained and rained, and tore the earth apart.
I then read on Abraham, Isaac and Jacob,
And how when people got married, they never did breakup
I read about Moses, how he talked kind of slow,
But told the Pharaoh let let let my my people go.

I felt a little tired and started to yarn,
But got revived when I read thru the book of Psalms.
I read about David sleighing the giant,
And how God's people always did triumph.
And read about Jonah, in the belly of a whale,
And the wicked king's wife, name Jezebel.
I read on Sarah, Rahab, and Ester,
And how God used women and continued to bless 'em
I read about priest, prophets and kings,
Just glories of stories and all sought of things,
I read about love, passion, desire,
And those three little boys that was thrown in that fire.
I looked at my watch it was ten forty three,
I got some egg nog and cookies and continue to read.

I read the Gospel of Matthew, Mark then Luke,
And the story of Judas, but that wasn't cute.
I read about Peter, John and James,
And being baptized in Jesus name
I read about Paul and all of his letters,
I kept reading and reading, it got better and better,
I then read Hebrews, Titus and Jude,
It was December 24th, and I was just in the mood.

But as I was reading, I said I must have missed it
Because the bible didn't say nothing about Christmas.
Well now I getting mad, my mind wouldn't trust it,
Back to old testament into the book of Judges.
On Eli, on Deborah, on Gideon, on Samson,
I read thru the all, but couldn't find an answer.
I read the books of Solomon, he suppose to be wise,
Well was Jesus really born on December Twenty Five?
And what about the wise men, they brought Jesus a gift,
And you mean to tell me it wasn't December Twenty Fifth?
So what's the hype about, if there shouldn't be any?
Must be the Wal-Mart, or JC Penny.
Well now I'm really mad, my mind is just a storming,
Cause ain't nobody getting a gift tomorrow morning.

I heard a voice from above, I said who can that be?
I don't believe in Santa, and I don't have a chimney.
The voice said I'm the Christ, the one born in a manger,
And you should know my voice, unless you are a stranger.
He said calm down, get back into the book,
I said Lord I read it once, he said take another look.
Look how I was born, like how I grew,
Read how I came and brought salvation unto you.
Read how I lived, picture how I died,
Bloodied on a cross, I hung crucified.
Read how on the third day, of how I rose again,
And I coming back to judge the world,
And yet I wont tell you when.

Read what I love, read what I hate,
And please don't focus on one simple date,
But give me all the Glory, give me all the Praise,
On December twenty fifth, and all the other days.
I said yes Lord I will, for my spirit does receive,
This Word from the Lord, in my home on Christmas eve.
I have peace in my mind, and calm in my storm,
Egg nog and cookies, and communion with the Lord,
So why the world is shopping running around like survival
I was home Christmas eve, just reading my bible.

Raymond K. Huff

LILLY OF THE VALLEY

ONE YEAR AGO TODAY

One year ago today, Life offered me the most,
Family, friends and loved ones, And you and I was so close.
We celebrated July 4th, with laughter in our heart,
With a bond of growing closer, And not growing apart.

But then a sudden phone call, the death of my friend,
My life seemed to change, from what was happening then.
Down the highway we raced, separate car and separate way,
Which changed the roads of life, ever since that day.

We should have had more time, but somehow time got lost,
As I look up towards the sky, No fireworks going off.
Having thoughts of my life, with the blueprints on a shelf,
The story I didn't read, the story of myself.
How you wanted more, I wasn't sure where it was,
I left my questions blank, and answered just because.
But that was no kind of answer, it was more like a myth,
As my life changed its course, the afternoon of July fifth.

We grew farther apart, and went thru different things,
But I still held belief, that our joy bells would ring.
Would ring loud with music, and you and I would dance,
Our paths would cross again, and we'd have a second chance.
But you never came back to me, I never held you tight,
Our passion seemed to fade, into the shadows of the night.
The ride abruptly stopped, an unexpected end,
The love we shared together, and the death of my friend.

But yet I thank God, for the time that we shared,
For I know within my heart, we were two hearts that cared.
So here on July fifth, I take the time to say,
I wish I could go back, One year ago today.

Raymond K. Huff

(Dedicated to Patrice, and the late Michael Moore)

Derived From: 2 Corinthians 5:17 Therefore if any man be in Christ, he is a new creature: old things are passed away; behold, all things are become new.

HAPPY NEW ME

I don't have to wait til January first,
To start a new chapter, to live a brand new verse.
But today I will be, happy, glad, and free.
Happy New Year starts today, with a brand new happy me.

I will not dwell, on the pains of my past,
For what made me cry, will now make me laugh,
For I am healed of my hurt, no matter what others say,
For like the sun I rise, and I rise this very day.

A man and woman came together, and they became my parents,
And that's whom God used, to bring on this planet.
So no matter if they were, good to me or not,
I've got to live, and utilize what I got.

For I got a life, and I got a choice,
I got a vision, and I got a voice,
I make the decision, to be happy as I can be.
And it starts today, with a brand new happy me.

No longer will I be mad, from the paths that I have came,
What is loss, is loss, but look what I have gained,
I have gained some knowledge, wisdom and power,
That has kept me thru the years, up to this very hour.

So I will not blame the others, about failures in my life,
For all things work for good, for all those who love Christ,
For he has changed my life, and he has set me free,
It's a happy new year, cause it's a happy new me.

Raymond K. Huff

BRAND NEW HAPPY ME :0)

Derived from: Job 10:19
I should have been as though I had not been; I should have been carried from the womb to the grave.

NOT MY WAY

If I had it my way, I never would have felt pain,
I never would know, the heavy storms of rain,
I would not have been hurt, to the point where I cried,
For the day that I was born, would have been the day I died.
That's how it would have happened if I did it my way.

If I had my way, God would have changed his mind,
A complete different path, he would have allowed me to find,
A path with no drama, a path with no stress,
The first air in my lungs, would have been my very last breath.
I would not deal with all this, if I chose my own path.

For when I came out, of my mothers womb,
They would have taken me, straight to the tomb,
It would have been better, to live a shorter life,
Than to go thru, such great sacrifice,

But if heaven is my final resting place,
Then I will endure, and finish out my race,
And all the praise, to God I will give,
That ignored my way, and allowed me to live.
He let me live thru the pain, Appreciate sunshine and rain,
Knowing I had so much to gain, so I no longer complain.

For he knew I could make it, he knew I would win,
Victory is mine, and it's all because of him,
Now I want to live, I want to breathe again,
And reach out to the Lord, like I reach out to a friend.

So I've learned to praise him, in the place where I cried,
And I've learned to live, where I wished I had died,
And now look forward to another day,
And surrender to God's will, and not my way.

Raymond K. Huff

Derived From: Hebrews 12:16-17 Lest there be any fornicator, or profane person, as Esau, who for one morsel of meat sold his birthright. 17 For ye know how that afterward, when he would have inherited the blessing, he was rejected: for he found no place of repentance, though he sought it carefully with tears.

TEARS OF ESAU

He is a man crying,
Inside he is slowly dying,
So out of pains and fears,
He repents to God with his tears,
But he doesn't find forgiveness

He knows that he has sinned,
He knows he has done wrong,
His life is filled with blues,
And he sings a sad sad song,
But still doesn't move God

He sold his appointed birthright,
For something mere to eat,
And now walks in depression
And a curse under his feet.

There is no light to guide him,
Life is dark and drear,
And the salt that's upon his lips,
Is the taste of his own tears.

He cries, and cries,
For the thing he has done,
He cries for repentance,
But yet he finds none.

For what is done in a moment,
Can set you back for years,
And even though you're sorry,
You could be crying with Esau tears.

Raymond K. Huff

MY HEART LOVED YOU FIRST

Before I touched your hand, Before I caressed your skin,
My heart had a plan, and held it deep within.
I could not write the next chapter, Could not predict every verse.
But I knew our love would last, because my heart loved you first.

My heart perceived my destiny, before my mind ever knew,
That I was so in love, with this person in my view,
And when two hearts beat together, and know how they feel,
Your visions become so clear, and your dreams become so real
I once hesitated to see if I would be hurt,
But I trust the love we have, and I value all its worth.

I've had pains in my past, hurt, tears and sorrow,
But I left them yesterday, in search of my tomorrow.
A tomorrow filled with love, where skies are blue not gray,
And I declare I will enjoy the sunshine of that day.
People have filled the world, and stars the universe,
But I would gladly tell them all, my heart loved your first

For life is worth living, when love has come in your life,
It strengthens you for your journeys, and heals you of pains and
strife.
For your love has become my medicine, your love has caused me
to heal,
I am whole and I am free, and I love how you make me feel.

I can now climb my mountain, I can now cross my bridge,
For love has made me alive, and I know how to live.
Just breathe, just breathe, exhale and now in,
With the comfort of a lover, and the company of my friend.

To hold you, to smell you, to see, taste or touch,
Was not needed for me to know, that I loved you so very much
Before we became intimate, before we became sexual,
Our hearts had come together, and their beats became
perpetually
And the music that we made, could not have been rehearsed,
A sweet melody of passion, where my heart loved you first.

I know that every thing good, comes from up above,
So I am so very grateful, to have you and love.
For surely as our God, created the heavens and earth,
I knew our love would last, because my heart loved your first.

Raymond K. Huff

TODAY I THINK

Today makes me think, of where I've been and women I've loved,
And Heavenly gifts I have received from above.

Today makes me think, of how life is so short,
And the lessons I've learned, and the lessons I've taught.

Today makes me think, of people I've known,
And those who were kids, are now all grown.

So as I think, and reminisce,
I get pictures in mind of days like this.

These pictures create, several questions within,
Like the meaning of life, and the love of a friend.

How blessed I am, that I have met you,
On this crowed planet, where friends are few,

So though it's Valentines Day, when love ones are pared,
And gifts, card, and candy are the materials shared.

But I have no gift, no candy, or card,
Just a mere thought without any regard,

That you are special, and a true friend of mine,
You are in my thoughts, as a dear Valentine.

Raymond K. Huff

(Written on Valentines Day for a friend far away)

TODAY I THINK

Derived From: Psalm 73:25 Whom have I in heaven but you? And earth has nothing I desire besides you (NIV)

I ONLY WANT GOD!

I knew I wanted something, but could not decide what it was,
So I looked throughout heaven and earth,
To find the one thing most needed in my life
Until the day of my death, since the time of my birth.

For it had to be something that would never leave me,
Something or someone who could truly understand,
It had to be able to endure the trying times,
And to know my body and spirit, my purpose and my plans.

Then a path appeared to me, it was like a opened window,
Right in front of me it became an open door.
And the thing that I desired, was not something new,
But it was like something, I beheld before.

It was the Presence of God, he led me, he guided me,
He talked me thru the hard times, he was always there in front,
He knew what was best for me, when I was undecided,
And I must admit, who knows exactly what I want.

But God was just a spirit, or a voice I heard from within,
But I wanted more of God, and needed more to see,
And like a mystery easily solved,
Without any shred of evidence,
God appeared tangible and visible to me.

Yes, he has revealed himself to me, He is not only a spirit,
And he is not a mere thought of my mind,
He is real, he is my friend, I don't have to defend,
For he was with me all the time.

I just needed faith to see him, I needed to want him in my life,
And to those who lack faith, this seems so very odd,
But for him I will sacrifice all other desires,
From Heaven above, to earth and below,
The thing I want most,
Is God.

Raymond K. Huff

Derived From: <u>2 Kings 20:1</u> In those days was Hezekiah sick unto death. And the prophet Isaiah the son of Amoz came to him, and said unto him, Thus saith the LORD, Set thine house in order; for thou shalt die, and not live.

LORD, A LITTLE MORE TIME

I hear I am going to die, so many things rush thru my mind,
I must take care of this and that, oh Lord, I need a little more
time.

Time to say good-bye to loved ones, time to smoothen out my
borders,
Time to forgive my enemies, and to get my house in order.

I knew this day would come, when the sun would no longer
shine,
I thought I would be ready, but Lord, I need a little more time.

Time to cleanse my heart, time to make sure I am saved,
To prepare my soul for eternity, and my flesh for it's grave.

Lord, I have walked upright, and loved you with soul, heart and
mind,
But to get my house in order, I need a little more time.

I will use my time wisely, and won't waste another day,
For once I see tomorrow, I will no longer have today.

So let me purify my soul, cleanse my heart and mind,
And thank God for his mercy, and giving me a little more time.

Raymond K. Huff

ONLY WISHED

Never meant to bring you pain, never meant to bring you sorrow,
just hoped time and time again, somehow we would find tomorrow.

A tomorrow filled with laughter, a time of happiness and joy,
where our hearts would be filled with love, like a kid with a
Christmas toy.

But tomorrow seemed so far, without directions from today,
within the midst of the fog, we somehow lost our way.

Your paths became entangled, mine was busy and strange,
two hearts that once felt loved, somehow began to change.

I heard what you were crying for, while dealing with your fears,
but my world had to be repaired, before I could dry your tears.

What started off with God, and prayer on our first date,
somehow was turned to hell, and salvation is a little too late.

I don't wish to go back, and change what was done,
I just wish I wake tomorrow, and feel the warmth of the sun.

To feel your love within me, to know our love is right,
but the love we shared in the day, has been lost during the night.

I wished we could have made it, until this life's end,
I wished you could of have remained, my lover and my friend.

But wishes are for people, that gaze upon a star,
not making destiny happen, but accepting the way things are.

But I thought we'd last forever, look back and reminisce,
how we'd lived out our dreams, but it's all just a wish.

Raymond K. Huff

AND GOD MOVED UPON THE WATERS...

Derived from: Esther 4:16 ... and fast ye for me, and neither eat nor drink three days, night or day: I also and my maidens will fast likewise; and so will I go in unto the king, which is not according to the law: and if I perish, I perish.

WHERE YA GOING?

Hey Ester where ya going? Where ya going Ester?
What? What? What? You're going to see the king?
What? What? Ester you know you can't go see the king.
Because don't nobody, just walk up to see the king
So Ester I pray, you don't do that thing.
You go see the king, and all his men will laugh,
Then throw you in a dungeon, or cut your body in half.
And if you sneak into his courts, you know you won't get far,
Their gonna get you girl, cause you'll be breaking the law.

So where ya going, where ya going Ester, come on tell me the truth,
I know that you're the queen, but honey you ain't Ruth.
So if you're going to see the king, I suggest you wait,
Besides Mordecia is already at the gate.
He's down there crying and begging, and talking to his friends,
Sitting in sathcloth and ashes, and they still won't let him in.
And you gonna go walk in, you gonna drive them men crazy,
Cause most of them think women, should just be cooking and having babies.
And you remember queen Vashti, and what the king had said,
So if you go walking in, you'll be d-e-a-d dead.

So where ya going, where ya going Ester? What, what tell me, where ya going?
You're going to see the king, because you say you got,
To go and talk to the king, and ruin Haman's plot.
So tell Mordecai to come home, and don't beg another day,
But to sanctify a fast, and the rest of us just pray.

So gather the fastest horses, and hook them to the chariot,
Cause you're going to see the king, and if you perish let you
perish.
So your trust is in the lord, and your standing on your faith,
That you will see the king, and God's people will be saved.
Well go on girl, do what you gotta do,
I'll stay here and fast, and say a prayer too.

And after you return, and you have succeeded,
Haman's plan we be destroyed, and the enemy defeated,
So thank God for the men, and what they're called to do,
But let's also thank God, for the women he called too.
And while were thanking God, and praising all day long,
Were gonna have a celebration and sing the queen a song.
So let the land rejoice, and the people sing,
Ester's going, Ester's going, going to see the king

Raymond K. Huff

Derived From: <u>Mark 8:33</u> But when he had turned about and looked on his disciples, he rebuked Peter, saying Get thee behind me, Satan: for thou sayest not the things the be of God, but the things that be of men.

GET BEHIND ME

There are some places I have to go,
There are some things I have to do,
A cross that I must bear,
Although you don't want me to.

So you try to interfere, because you don't understand,
You speak not the words of God, but you speak the words of man
So get behind me...

For man doesn't see, as the Lord can see,
Man has no words, that can set the weary free.
For you see my ugly cross, and you try to keep me down,
But look beyond the cross, and you can see my crown.
But as for now, get behind me.

For I just appointed you, to be part of my works,
And now you want to rebuke me, and now cause me hurt.
What about my purpose, what about my cup,
What about long-suffering, isn't that a part of love?
And if I cannot overcome, the trials made for me,
Then my life is incomplete, and I've missed my destiny.
So please, get behind me.

I know you mean me well, and you want to heal and cure,
But some things in life, that we all must endure.
For I know you are my friend, and don't want to see me go
But if you can't accept God's will for me, then you have become
my foe.

So I cannot allow your love, to go against the plan,
That was designed for me, before the world began.
So please hold your hurt, your pain and your sorrow,
For you too have a cross, so pick it up and follow.
And remember stay behind me.

Raymond K. Huff

THE RIGHT PATH

Written For a Friend at her Fortieth Birthday Celebration

COMPARING FORTY

Life can be hot, warm, cool or cold,
So I took a little time, wrote this rhyme,
To compare life at forty years old.

Now just because you're forty, don't start feeling blue,
Because you're younger than a lot of people here,
But you're older than a lot of people too.

See forty is a number, that can be fun or quite serious,
It's the same number of days, that Jesus was in the wilderness.

And I know you been thru some things, and the devil has been
messin'
But after you come thru forty, tell the devil "Get the Steppin!"

Now forty is also the years, the Israelites had to spend,
Walking in a circle, and just wondering.
Where is this thing that God has promised to me?
Where is my land? My milk and my honey?
But I'm sure you have changed your clothes,
And I'm sure you have changed your shoe,
So therefore you're no Israelite, and this part ain't about you.
I am just comparing something to forty.

But I am sure you have some things, that the Lord has promised,
And since God cannot lie, it will surely be accomplished!

Cause after forty years, I'm sure your reminisce
Where you been, and where your at, and what's coming after
this.

Long as the earth remains, there will be seed time and harvest,
So no matter what comes your way, hold your head up regardless.

And have peace in your spirit, and joy in your soul,
Knowing the Lord above, let you see forty years old.

HAPPY BIRTHDAY

Raymond K. Huff

NINTH DAY OF MAY

When God was making Beauty,
He knew just what to do,
On the Ninth day of May,
The Lord above made you.

He gave you a beautiful spirit,
Made you a lovely sight to see,
For you are truly wonderful,
And you're beautiful to me.

So let's give God Praise,
For making you this way,
Happy Birthday unto you,
On the Ninth Day of May,

Raymond K. Huff
(Dedicated to Brenda)

ANOTHER YEAR GOD HAS KEPT ME

I GOTTA WAKE UP

I was so happy to be with you,
It was like a dream come true,
But now the time is over, the alarm has sounded,
And I gotta wake up.

I was so glad we came together,
I prayed it would last forever,
But forever came much to soon,
And now I gotta wake up.

I loved you so strong,
So I will cry all night long,
And in the morning, with tears on my pillow.
You will be gone,

My dream is over,
Final Good-bye's
Hope to see you later,
When I wake up.

Raymond K. Huff
(Dedicated to those who's loved one past)

Written for a two women who gave me information, so I could write about their sister.

I explained to their sister, I wrote based on the info received, but…

YOU CAN CLARIFY THE FACTS

Your family had an idea, and called me on the phone,
Said, "Can you use your poetic talents, and write a little poem?"
They told me a little this, and they told me a little that,
I put it all together, but you can clarify the facts.

They said you were born, into a wonderful family,
The best parents in the world that there could ever be.
Said you had two sisters, your parents had only girls,
And your the third best child, they have in this world

They said that your father, has a voice that should be heard,
He can't only spank a butt, but he can preach a mighty word.
Your mother's his favorite member, wearing those fancy hats,
Now this is what they told me, but you can clarify the facts.

They said about fifteen years ago, back in '92
You came running to the alter, and the Holy Ghost got in you.
You repented of your sins, all of those evil days,
Gave your life to the Lord, and changed your wicked ways.
Now I'm not saying you were wicked, and they didn't tell me that,
It just fit in with the poem, but you can clarify the facts.

They said you like to sing, and you like to sing,
And you really like to sing, about almost anything.
They said you can really sing, and I should hear you sing,
And there's an anointing on your life, to sing praises to the King.
I said does she sound like Whitney? They said I better get it right,
With Val on the keyboard, and your sister on the mic.
The three of you have a sound, that is truly heaven sent,

98

Make a preacher wanna cry, and make the devil repent.
They told me some more of this, and little more of that,
I just write and recite, but you can clarify the facts.

They say your mom's your best teacher, your dad is your favorite
preacher,
You had a friend who moved away, and now it's hard to reach her.
You can be a church greeter, but you are a worship leader,
And if you saw a hungry soul, you would have to feed her.
You're a natural born leader, you hate liars and all cheaters,
You enjoy watching a real good movie, but you hate scary
creatures.
The Lord is your shepherd, your guide and your leader,
You worked hard to get your Masters Degree, and now you are a
teacher.
This is what they told me, little this and little that,
I wrote this poem on my own, but you can clarify the facts.

So no matter what you go, no matter what you do,
Here is a part of the poem, that I know is certainly true.
They planned this event, and nice birthday surprise,
To bring happiness to your heart, and tears of joy to your eyes.
To put money in your hand, and gifts upon your lap,
They did this because they love you, and that is a fact.

Raymond K. Huff

DANCE STEPS OF LIFE

This poem is dedicated to a friend,
Who is a daughter, a sister, mother and wife,
A person who have been anointed by God,
And how he has guided, her dance steps of life.

She has anointed parents, who raised her in the Lord,
And who taught to know right from wrong,
She thought that she would live with them forever,
That was until Mr. Right came along.

We watched how they dated, then fell in love,
So now she was dancing to a wedding beat,
Later she announced they were gong to have a baby,
Then she had to dance with two swollen feet.

So this once sprinting track star had to slow down
For her lovely children, to whom she'd given birth,
Now this dancer, has become a mother,
God's gift to her, thru her to earth.

But don't stop the music, don't stop the beat,
There's more in store, for this dancer's feet.

She is a worshipper and a youth leader,
Church administrator and a prophetess too,
Anything she can do to help
She is always willing to do.

But the steps of life flow throughout the land,
And they are not confined to the church,
All throughout school, and even thru college,
And even the place where she currently works.

She has become a God appointed light,
Shining bright for all to see,
So we gathered today for we want to say,
Congratulations on your Masters Degree.

Dear friend, dear sister, daughter, mother and wife,
May the Lord keep guiding your dance steps of life.

Raymond K. Huff

GOD RAISED A MAN

I have had the pleasure, to see God's created land,
I have been truly blessed, to see God's orchestrate a plan,
I have seen his tender mercies, and the strength of his hand,
And today I like to say, I seen God raise a man.

So glory be to God, unto him we give praise,
For Brother Vernon Warren, the man God has raised.

God kept him as a child, in this dangerous city no doubt,
And protected him from the enemy, keeping him safe in God's
house.
Where he loved to play the drums, you could see his joy inside,
Then he'd jump up and praise God, by doing the Vernon slide.

Slide Vernon Slide, Give Praise to your God.

In a city where many men, turn to violence and drugs,
God raised such a man, who is gentle as a hug.
A man who is affectionate, loving and caring too,
Who seeks the path of peace, in all that he may do.

But oh no, he is not soft, not weak nor immature,
He is firm, but he is fair, and values what is pure.

So slide Vernon Slide, slide much as you can,
I confess we are blessed, to see God raise a man.

He loves happy times, like a kid with a Christmas toy,
He is a family man, and that's his pride and joy.
He has been strengthened by the Lord, in soul, mind and heart,
And knows how to hold together, when things are falling apart.

He's and artist and a chef, and a crazed sports fan
Who knows how to make the bacon, and fry it in the pan.
He is a dedicated father, still in the house of God,
A hard working man, who can still do the slide.

So happy 40th birthday, for you will give God praise,
To Brother Vernon, The man that God has raised.

Written By Raymond K. Huff

On behalf of Naomi to Vernon

I pray this book has been a blessing for you to read,
Much as it has been a blessing to me to write.
I give all Praise and Thanks to my Lord Jesus Christ,
For his goodness and mercy unto me.

Evangelist Raymond K. Huff

I Give Praise To My Lord And Savior Jesus Christ For His
Blessings Unto Me
Amen